OLD-FASHIONED
Love and Romance

A PICTORIAL ARCHIVE FROM
NINETEENTH-CENTURY
SOURCES

Selected and Arranged by

CAROL BELANGER GRAFTON

Dover Publications, Inc., New York

Copyright

Copyright © 1989 by Dover Publications, Inc.
All rights reserved under Pan American and International Copyright Conventions.

Published in Canada by General Publishing Company, Ltd., 30 Lesmill Road, Don Mills, Toronto, Ontario.
Published in the United Kingdom by Constable and Company, Ltd., 3 The Lanchesters, 162–164 Fulham Palace Road, London W6 9ER.

Bibliographical Note

Old-Fashioned Love and Romance: A Pictorial Archive from Nineteenth-Century Sources is a retitled (1994) reprint of the work originally published by Dover Publications, Inc., in 1989 as *Love and Romance: A Pictorial Archive from Nineteenth-Century Sources*.

DOVER *Pictorial Archive* SERIES

Library of Congress Cataloging-in-Publication Data

Old-Fashioned love and romance : a pictorial archive from nineteenth-century sources / selected and arranged by Carol Belanger Grafton.
   p.   cm. — (Dover pictorial archive series)
   ISBN 0-486-25938-2
   1. Drawing—19th century. 2. Love in art. 3. Erotic art. I. Grafton, Carol Belanger. II. Series.
   NC90.L68   1989
   760′.04428′09034—dc19   88-27241
                                                                          CIP

Manufactured in the United States of America
Dover Publications, Inc., 31 East 2nd Street, Mineola, N.Y. 11501

Publisher's Note

The nineteenth century was, perhaps, the great era for the depiction of the sentimental approach to love and romance. Women were placed on the loftiest of pedestals, and the ritual of courtship was extremely elaborate. To aid graphic artists and those needing material with a romantic touch, Carol Belanger Grafton has sifted through rare magazines, books and printed ephemera of the nineteenth century (with occasional forays into earlier and later periods) to present almost every aspect of the topic through the ages, in settings as diverse as the dining table and playing field (as well as the more obvious locale of the boudoir). Keen-eyed readers will recognize the hand of such noted artists as Charles Dana Gibson and James Montgomery Flagg. All the pictures are rendered in the crisp black and white that is a hallmark of the period.

3

11

19

24

34

Reugeron Vignerot SC

36

Rougeron Vignerot. sc

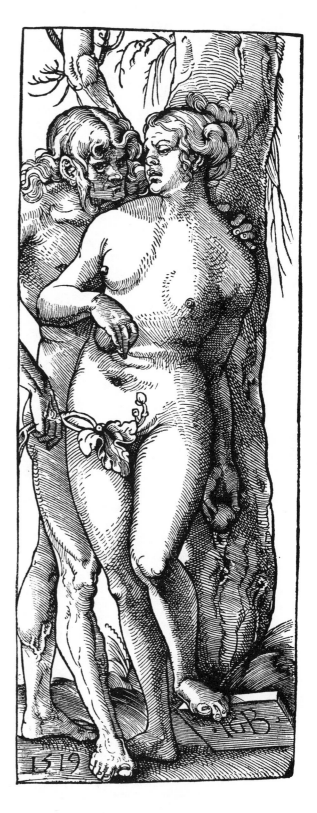

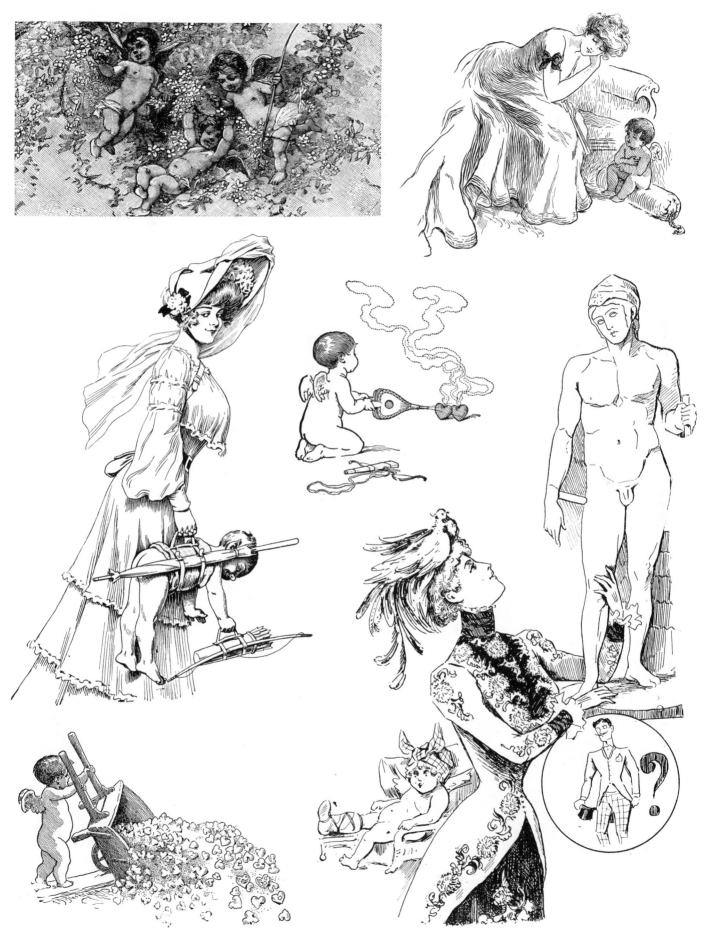

98

Roupeton, Vignerot, Demoulin sc.

104